To Dari,

I hope you enjoy this
wee pamphlet — sending
you hawthorn wishes from
Scotland,

Le grá
Éadaoin

Published by Nine Pens

2022

www.ninepens.co.uk

ISBN: 978-1-7398274-6-5

014

I inclined
To lose my faith in Ballyrush and Gortin
'Til Homer's ghost came whispering to my mind.
He said: I made the Iliad from such
A local row. Gods make their own importance.

—from Patrick Kavanagh, 'Epic'

Otherwise I might have well
ignored the ground that shone for me, that did enough
to make itself rebound from me, out of which I was
made.

—from Medbh McGuckian, 'Isba Song'

Aflame

After Methuselah star

First light. Blue, like a kingfisher, an old bruise, leaky
ink. Burning at cosmic degrees, scalding edge

of fire, licking hairs that flare and grow
ice blue. Shine. Flash. Burn.

It came after matter, before life. And just like that,
the universe was not opaque.

We should all be pyromaniacs.
We come from the same fire.

Baby blue. Colour of Dad's eyes. Foamy tide. I learn
that blue comes from fire, word and otherwise.

A flame that crackles in other words—*lucid,
illustration, leukaemia, Lucifer*.

Azure and ultramarine come from lapis;
lapis, cobalt, sapphire, from fire;

cerulean, aquamarine, the sea;
the sea from stars. Stars, from fire.

Homer had no word for blue, only

'wine-dark.' Play drunk in spacetime.

I see more than I think, off puddles, tiles,
glass, eyes, skin; how it makes us transparent,

mercurial. If light has a sound, it is thunder.
Plants. Spitting oil. Batteries. Birdsong.

Each sliver of life we live bears heat. I feel a meaning
in every gesture. Then, none.

My skull is full of earth, facts drifting down like snow.
Light began, and it began blue. We are made of finite fire,

of brightness, exposure, eclipse. Every time I bake bread
it is a vast improbability. We are all a flame.

On the sea wall in Lahinch, the Atlantic breaks
again. I bleed into blue at the water's edge.

Boireann

Exposed as the crown of a balding head, the Burren persists. For years
life has been scraped off clints, pulled by the teeth from grikes,
and even now the rocky place turns hard going into milk and cream.

Its great stage has seen more aging than this—mollusc and ammonite riveted
in its face as fossils. Your feet grace an ocean floor carved by glacial ice,
but this rock sinks so deep no water can follow. Archives of abandoned living.

Wind covers the Burren with its breath and on rare days, it lifts.
On rare days, it lifts. Like a rest in music, a note suspended
Between one bow stroke and the next.

Trees fail in six inches of topsoil, leaving whittled thickets and hollowed crowns
bent double on ancient stone. Shelter to fairy folk. As if they do not age, they simply lean
further down. Our rhythm is a dance through the branches.

I stand at the edge of Dún Aengus, close to the brink of awe and terror, a deep wheel
that comes to a stop—I lose gravity in that sudden drop, that creeping freefall, before I
sleep. For now it's no more than a minor key, pulled from my mind like roots.

Our music was born from the landscape.
Phrasing, the way the stresses fall, is how we move along the limestone,
living between one bow stroke and the next.

Knot

Grief is in the weather, when water thickens
over limestone and floods us, when hurt
closes in like heavy air and the turlough swells,
rippling out over county lines. My auntie tells me
how the swell came to her brother, how it put them
in a car going nowhere. The air rises in me as I hear her
tell it, water table fluctuates: these stories only arrive
once, shucked from memory and prized
as they appear in my hands. I can see the water
in them, racing by the car, attempting
to outrun deluge. They drove for hours, no mind
of where, until they stopped in Sneem—if ever there was
an end of the world. Sneem. So remote it's named for a knot,
the last thing to tie us to land. Nothing there for them
but being somewhere else. She does not tell me
what they did or what was said. I watch the water
flow between us, mirror-sharp, and then disappear,
while I'm dammed in, thinking of Sneem.

Huathe: Hawthorn

⊣

Blowing through teeth of a drystone wall,
the gale, *gaoithe*, summons a sea behind it,
making scraw of the hawthorn. Better than
a fairy wind, compassed by terrible quiet,
this screeching air twists hawthorn askew
in dense gnarls that crease the sky. Wind
intersects their upward glance,
a perfect three cross-roads. *Gaoithe*
is wise, teaching the briar its name,
sceach gheal, hiding thorns beneath
its blossoms. Fissures in the wood
appear with age, wrinkles like scars,
and do not die, even when that scent
is on its petals.

　　　　　What sharp ache
brought someone to a fairy tree
and dare touch it, skin its skin,
pluck its fruit, tear its leaves?
Bound in to briars, petals frozen,
waiting for the wind. Pierced in the side
with hope, until the air was silent.

Study of Bread

Who'd have thought this bread made from Mungoswells flour and Maldon salt
and olive oil and instant yeast would turn out so well? Who knew to make

so much of wheat, and fruit, and the sea? I pour oil on my hands and slide
my fingertips in when the dough is ready to prove itself and the bubbles loosen

air from this living thing, like burping a baby, but the bubbles rarely pop.
They stiffen in the heat of the oven and go soft when they cool.

I have seen the sugars browning on the crust, their molecules sighing
oh-oho-ho while they rise. Somewhere in Ireland my mother is making

shortcrust and I still can't do it, no matter how often she shows me.
So I bake bread. I've learned that salt is not just a flavour,

but strengthens from within, makes the dough elastic.
I've been eating bread for years: soda bread, brown bread, ciabatta, rye,

brioche, pita, naan, sourdough, baguette, tortilla, challah and more,
and never knew that salt made it pliant. I would flick it on the hot range

as a child to hear the crackling noise, throw it over my shoulder for luck,
taste it when I swallowed seawater, rub it into meat and not think of the animal.

I should call home, before the timer rings.

Orbis Alius / Other World

> An island means isolation; the words are the same.
> —Louis MacNeice, *I Crossed the Minch*

On the OS map, marking the Clare-Galway border,
is the Church of Duagh's son, Saint Colman,
whose girdle dropped on the spot where he fell

to work, and live, and die, in a time of miracles. The map
of course cannot show the lichened drystone wall
or the local belief that lying on the Saint's grave can cure pain

or even the lure of near-forgotten myth:
Loch a'Bhaidhte, lake of the overflowing,
hides away the tower bell,

thrown in desperation or fear by a monk
in an age of terrors. Now, the clapper is eaten away
by hard water, the soundblow crusted to limestone.

The tower base walls are thick enough to bed a man,
just as they have buried them,
and ten feet above the ground is a gap in the stone,

the front door. All year it is exposed
to *Gort* and *gaoithe* but closed to those
who know not how to enter.

Dusk reveals its austere beauty when each fallen corner
of the church, tombs, ruins, fills black contours
on the pink sky – rough as islands,

but they are just circles on the map, gradients of elevation,
like rocks in water, rippling, soundless,
alone. *Oileáin*.

Anam

How to tell this name has lived longer
than the written word, louder than the breath,
the sigh, the hiss, and bitter curse put on Étain —

forebearer and bloodless ancestor become a fly
at the wind's mercy, cast on the rocks, consumed
with a goblet of wine, reborn, not redeemed:

a first wife's scorn, identified, taxonomied,
and filed away as jealous passion.
What nomenclature this name is,

my soul inscribed with another's dissolution
word broken down and dissolved to atom incarnate
as saints & scholars writing an epic of wooing

swallow the diacritics and offer critique.
I am raging, rampaging, lithic: where my soul
purpose and feeling are [deadname].

Olympus came to Tara and I have never been the same,
seeking imperfect safety at home in limestone, too soft:
barely scratching strength above talc or gypsum.

I have been a poet, a swan, a deity, a queen,
yet dispossessed — digested in mouths of men
who felt they could tell the story better.

I am drawn to the rocks that wrecked her, the wine
that trapped us, the passion that named me,
and how easy it is to leave a mark.

> it is sweet
> to taste resilience
> to be beyond salvation

Fierce scrow

body (n.)
from Old English 'Bodig,' meaning '[a man's] chest,'
extended to denote a person's form in later 13th century

Adam's rib and a calcium breath are not the truth.
I found hope there; calcite deposits in a dank cave
have more relevance, stalactite antiques hanging
hollow over shifting ground. Chesty origins seem
fitting when I cannot fit into body made from a hidden word,
sound created from a parenthesis of agendas,
shaped from a man long forgotten, renamed, reborn,
like Eve, scapegoated into submission.
My body has proved a part-time living, fig-leafed
with troubled language, blooming
from a man's chest, a woman's womb, a woman's biblical
misunderstanding: living proof my form is
manlier than most. Broad shoulders, butch
reclining. The word *handsome* has beheld & held me,
its gloss subdividing into sense—*striking,*
imposing, substantial: how kind of the masculine
forms to make space for me.
Bone of my bone after all flesh of my flesh.

Break

I haven't taken this train in years.
When it stops at your station, no-one alights.

Rushing like a gale, my thoughts are late
all along the line. And there you are. Beaming,

unchanged. You even kiss the same.
You hold my hand, I meet your mother, and

my envious heart says, *this is it*.
When I think of you now, it's deliberate. And artefact.

Dried lavender, a box of untouchables, rolling microfiche
on a small display. I will never explain you properly,

so you seem more a mystery. It only happens in the dark.
In this world, Sappho's fragments are complete.

My heart says, *now here, enough*. These stories
are unfair. The river burst its banks again

and I can't ask if you were there,
if the house flooded, if the trinkets of us made it.

The river burst its banks and our photos,
ruined, drift out with the tide.

They wash up again each time I think they won't.

Dear Anne Lister

Tell me about Jacks, Anne, why
you dress all in black—your sixth sense for
desire, the sixth satire of Juvenal. We don't
speak but I'm full up with you and fit to
burst. Since you love & only love the fairer
sex, I'm happy you found them fresh as
pears for someone who had a taste for it.

I thought to take your top hat, tap
your cane, learn your crypthand while you
watch. Cyphers within your private
entries—there's nothing so bittersweet as
coded touch. Your kisses are legend. All the
places your mouth has been, & every word
you didn't say—these are my curriculum.
Tell me about M, who owns your heart but,
alas, has got the piles; or Tib, if the discharge
is venereal.

Penetrating looks, you were
waiting on ladies in waiting for men
to disappoint them. Do you still see yourself
in a man's guise, clothes, and body, too? For
you I want to wear all black, bind my chest
in a way you might despise, but for how you
sewed leather onto clean stays, laced into
hide and hiding, bound as tough outside as
you grew inwardly.

Maybe that is why you wrote in cypher about clothes, just as much as sex, of wearing drawers with men's waistcoat and braces. So many more have followed on, to tread the paths of Shibden with an oyster eye.

One day my heart will drop like a horseshoe and leave no trace but this. Until then I keep it hanging above the door.

Unction

two fingers slide into mouth

of me, for me

it is a gift

to be given back to myself

Botanical Gardens

Gardens bloom in all weather.
Bluebirds sang from bluebells
and terraced ivy rose to the clasp
of a stocking held to skin, suspended
between silk and stubbornness;
long tendrils and curled fingers
around the heart of a bulb
clothed dew-sweat and leaf-veins.
Beds of heather roughed bare touch,
fleshy petals fell hot and cold as wax
and thunder boomed over the hills.

Glór

The island is what we call the graveyard,
split on the brow of a hill, and rain sprints
from the ocean to wet her grave

on the far side of it. This visit
came five years late, along with myself.
Aprils come and go. Her vocal chords

grow into grass on the island, her last notes
wind brushing along the blades.
My childhood home is within sight,

though I travelled only to reach this point
for the very first time. I forgot flowers. I dwell here
like hot air over cold and a torn thought

enters my mind—what must she look like now,
a few feet beneath my feet? It hollows me out
like a bird bone, horizon careening too close.

Long years in London never left her voice.
I wonder how much she lived there,
in leather or in hiding, in the strikes, the riots—

violence like water on a grease fire. I knew
her just here, on limestone, voice clear
as a tuning fork. She had a spiral staircase

in her house. A room of guitars. It's gutted
now I pass it by. Her grave is simple,
looking east. I miss her most

when she sings inside my head. I never
asked why she never married, I never
knew in time. She was not old enough

for this. I laugh because
it's wrong to laugh,
and cry when it sounds like her.

Lost for any words she might hear
I start to pray. Sound of ocean wind,
Holy. Unkempt grass and gravel,

Holy. Algae blooms a comfort,
Holy. Walking away, its own prayer.
Holy. When I sing, she sings.

Maritime

Once they discovered pendulums do not keep time at sea,
they understood why the maps were off.
Without knowing the time at home
distance was unfathomable
and they knew first-hand the risk of watching the clock.

Munro in November

My first—surrounded by mist, doubled in the lake,
and my doubt living its ninth life that I would ever
reach the summit, heels chafing in my new boots,
and the woods falling away too soon as the ascent
began forty-five degrees in grey light before the sun
crested the mountain in birdsong I could not name
and cattle half-way up did not go as high as me when
I reached the first plateau, ran out of water,
and found no promised well, and dipped a flask
into little rivers trailing from the top and never tasted
it so clear, while people passed me out both ways
and I shamed to think of Nan the wick-slip
cavorting Cairngorms, of trig point selfies, of ease,
and ego wild with failure, and how much I hated my body.
And then—a hum. A hum hum hum. Screaming
knees and sweat in my eyes but a hum hum hum. Losing
daylight and shaky legs in a hum. If my head cracked open
on the mountain quartz all I could think would be hum.
And when I stumbled up the summit, I felt nothing.
I tell the story humbly, with grace, I trust it sounds
impressive. Because I fear and love the humming,
which has not left me since.

Dear Benny

After Quelques Corps Favorables No.3

A matter   of the heart
suspended   in weightless   motion

your   eight   stolen roses
are   perfect

Fresh   from the *vingtième*
petals like papier-mâché
against the portrait miniature:
Rembrandt   seems   affronted
though charmed
by my attention

Your latest creation has cut me
short
like secateurs through the stem
cambium   so close
to cardium

Longing for suspension
I see in your craft
a softness that lifts
a touch   tailored to solitude
so unexpected and so welcome

Adrift   in blank space

everything is illicit

I imagine your Paris and its sex shops
(desire is so French), replete with these
floral debutantes and red wine;
Baroque pavilions; phonemes my lips elide—
j'ai allumé le feu, mes chagrins, mes plaisirs—

My eye drifts   to the present
magnificent   pink   peonies
gracing the vase next to me
and I know   you would approve,
their bulbous, explicit   stamen on show,
naked   by the windows
for all the neighbours   peeking in

And we are all   weighted
with borrowed time

at a neolithic cairn

up late with fraught dreams
I went out to Poulawack
with a bad habit in hand I struck a match
and held close the card

watching the sun skim below horizon
I felt clandestine in this warmest
kindest immolation of blue
first light   and last

I pressed an impatient toe under a stone
and a word grew up from the dark to meet me
'diagnosis'
                              its roots in 'recognition'
stressing knowledge I did not have
and wouldn't concede
until the rage had left me (it has not left me still)

watching light fade was I thought relaxing
until I did it in too chill a breeze
thinking how mad I looked to the neighbours
who had not yet heard
but would soon come knocking with food

I had nearly done with all my notions
when I heard a piercing cry, a haunting screech

I could not place except for what I knew of banshees

harbingers of death
                        or high dramatics

as a nimble fox stepped through a gate and shrieked again

and never noticed me above
                        crying relief

Matchmaking at Madigan's

an old arrangement between patriarchs
follows tradition that if the river floods

marriage terms are to be
negotiated over the torrent

hammering out a settlement
above gushing waters

the place was the meeting
point of two townlands

chosen in the hope
it could be crossed

one day owned
and that their lives

would be more
than struggling

even to be heard

Reincarnation

The day we clear the old house, my Dad tries on a tie,
and walks to the wall where a mirror no longer hangs.
His eyes mist over as the room is too empty
of itself and too full of us. He goes to the car
and I fiddle with the mantlepiece clock out of time,
force the clicking gears to grind and rip until the face
is right. Suns and moons whizz past the window
up to the moment I close the glass door. Dad stands
alongside, says his mother would set it,
slow and delicate, like a prayer. I watch him
gently nudge the clock hands with his big fingers
& wonder how he fits them on a fiddle string & then
wonder at my own. My feet are cold from the floor,
its flagstones so tightly fit only a machine can lift them,
though only men laid them down. The house has more
stories than it can tell. Maybe that is why
the fuchsia does not die. In the clearing out, we find
an oval hand mirror, tarnished with age, and I take it.
Looking for lost relations between brass edges, I see
my brow & theirs. I am square in living memory,
walking back to future selves, my eyes
alighting on every one I already know.

Kicking the crate

Each night, I trust I will be here when I wake.
        That is, I choose to trust. Else I don't sleep.

Drifting between subconscious and unconscious,
        to fantasies of someone fictional

so long as the plot is robust (if it's well-met,
        pleasure is meticulous, though my own is grossly

impatient), I am startled by that thing I've almost
        forgotten, that – yes, I'll be dead.

Studying the war poets, I wondered why they wrote so much
        of desire; beyond Freud, I thought it immature,

a young lad's fresh freedom, adventure under crossfire.
        They toast their enamel mugs - a dull clunk

Death and sex. Two unknown unknowns, until they happen.
        As if desire were all that kept us alive.

And it is. I will never rest until I am laid, laid up, and at last
        laid down. I will be simplified.

The name for that falling feeling before sleep
        is a 'hypnic jerk': where the inner ear senses

your blood pressure decrease and your muscles relax
        but the eye is black to danger. You jerk awake

because your body is no more than your service animal.
        By living, you know how it feels to die.

All that calms me afterwards is the waking dream
        of getting everything I want. Almost.

Deora Dé

Too much of everything, between stone
walls you find seas of rushes, bogland, orchids, lush
grass, sometimes caves. Each place

named for a story—
the cairn, the horse's leap, church of the fertile hillside—
recorded assiduously in maladapted phonetics:

'The rectorial tithes, jointly with those of Clouney, are
compounded for £166 13s 4d., and are appropriated
to the deanery of Kilfenora.'

History is someone who
walked by the house yesterday, scattering elderflower
and ruins.

Census records ask if they could read or write,
but show they spoke two mother tongues, one born of home,
and one of necessity.

'Aillwee' means nothing, but *Aill Bhuí*
tells us we're at the yellow cliffs. It is said: *sceach gheal*,
hawthorn, brings bad luck, death resting on its blossoms.

If uprooted, gentians draw lightning. Four-leaf shamrocks grow wherever a mare foaled. So it goes—excavation only grazes the topsoil.

                              Flowers grow blue in this astringent earth. We don't know the meaning of the fuchsia by my grandfather's house, but it survived the winter that killed everything else.

Every summer it blooms a thousand brilliant sirens.

Notes

Fierce Scrow

A phrase native to North Clare, meaning an insatiable
zest for work/a compulsive work-drive.

'Boireann':

Irish (n.), 'The Burren,' a karst landscape & national
park in North Clare, incorporating a vast
cracked pavement of glacial-era limestone.
Literally 'great rock.'

'Knot':

Turlough – literally 'dry lake,' a feature of The
Burren, where apparent lakes will emerge
overground after heavy rains, with no natural surface
outlet — principally filled by subterranean waters —
and disappear again when the water table rebalances.

'Huathe':

Huathe – the name of the Ogham symbol, which
translates to 'H.' It also means 'hawthorn.'
Gaoithe – Irish, 'winds,' with an etymological root in
'wise.'
Sceach gheal – Irish, 'hawthorn.'

'Orbis Alius/Other World':

Orbis Alius – the realm of the dead in Celtic
mythology.

Gort – Irish, 'field' or 'meadow.' Also the name of the town closest to Kilmacduagh.

Gaoithe – Irish, 'winds,' with an etymological root in 'wise.'

Oileáin – Irish, 'islands.'

'Anam'

Irish (n.), from Latin 'anima,' meaning:

1. name
2. soul
3. liveliness, spirit; breath

This poem explores the myth of Étaín, from Tochmarc Étaíne (The Wooing of Étaín), one of the oldest and richest stories of Irish mythology, and in effect a patchwork of oral histories and Christian narratives amalgamated into polytheistic cosmology.

One of the many transformations that Étaín undergoes is being turned into a scarlet fly by her husband's jealous first wife, who then creates a wind and blows the fly away so Étaín cannot alight anywhere but the rocks of the sea for seven years. Étaín-as-fly later falls into a glass of wine, swallowed and reborn a millennium after her first birth.

'Glór'

Title name is Irish for 'voice,' 'speech,' or 'song.'

'Dear Benny':

> For Benny Nemer, Canadian-born artist and diarist, whose project 'Quelques Corps Favourables' imagines alternative approaches to art historiography and the forging of queer kinship bonds. This poem responds to No. 3, a work the artist addresses to his friend Conny. Available here:
> https://corpsfavorables.fr/Conny-English

'Kicking the crate'

> Title name taken from Peaky Blinders' main character Tommy Shelby (written by Steven Knight), describing his own panic and PTSD: 'Sometimes I'm a horse in a crate, just kicking the crate.'

'Deora Dé':

> Colloquial Irish for 'fuchsia,' literally translates to 'Tears of God.'
> The valuation cited refers to the townland Kiltoraght, and is taken from the Parliamentary Gazetteer of 1845, available on the Clare County Library website here:
> https://www.clarelibrary.ie/eolas/coclare/places/kiltoraght1845.htm

Acknowledgements

To Colin at Nine Pens: Thank you for taking this leap of faith. I'm so grateful.

In order of appearance in my life:

> My family – Sorry for the artistic license. Thank you for everything.

> Liz – I don't know where to start. But the rest of our lives sounds pretty good. I'm so lucky you're in mine.

> Annie, Caitlin, Han, SJ, and all my Starcourt loves – My chosen family.

> Rosa & Moss, Alexa & Justin, Bryn, Peter and Miriam – Words don't really do you any justice, and neither does 'thank you,' but thank you anyway, always.

> Mairi and Mystika – Thank you for believing in my work so much, on faith, that you offered a platform for me to share it. The way you support your communities is invaluable.

Josie and Darcy – For being as kind and welcoming as you are, and for all the work you do for your friends and communities, I'm really grateful.

Sophie, Rose & all Devotees, and The Poets Collective – These poems wouldn't exist without your encouragement and inspiration. Thank you from the Marianas Trench of my Taurean heart.

Dave and Padraig – Some of the best bits of Belfast. Thank you for reading this pamphlet in its earlier forms and for being so generous in your encouragement.

To Cathy McCormack † 12.4.2015.

To Eoin Ryan † 7.6.2011.

To the other 1,201,606 Irish people who voted 'Yes' in 2015 – You give me strength, every day.

Many thanks, finally, to those who first believed in this work:

- *Gutter Magazine* (Issue 26, Autumn 2022): 'Aflame' in its earlier form
- *The North* (Issue 68, August 2022): 'Study of Bread'
- *Elements: Natural and the Supernatural* (Fawn Press, 2021): 'Knot' and 'Huathe: Hawthorn,' as their younger selves
- *The London Magazine Poetry Prize* (2016): Shortlisting 'Orbis Alius / Other World'

Ingram Content Group UK Ltd.
Milton Keynes UK
UKHW040902170523
421883UK00003B/8